11-2013

Vickie

STINGS
OF M.S.

Author

Vickie [Long, Shortley] Berwaldt

Amazon.com

ISBN-10: 1480192597

EAN-13: 9781480192591

Library of Congress Control Number: 2012920463
CreateSpace Independent Publishing Platform
North Charleston, South Carolina

Dedication

*To Lynn, Dawn, and Bob. To Phil for giving me
the gentle nudge I needed to accomplish my dream,
and to Cecilia for planting the seed.*

Table of Contents

Foreword

I watched as my husband placed the tiny yellow bee on my arm. The bee fluttered its wings as it moved in for the most vulnerable spot. The bee's stinger penetrated my skin and injected its venom, causing piercing pain to pulse through my body. Through clinched teeth I cried, "Please, dear Lord, may this therapy work!"

Yes, I have MS (Multiple Sclerosis), and I've had it for over fifty years. This is (most often) a crippling and cruel disease that tries to consume the entire body; however, I have waged my own battle against MS. With God's help, I am determined to live my life to the fullest. I have raised a family and have married twice. In fact, Bob and I married just four years ago, and life together is great. Indeed, awesome.

Five hundred thousand people are diagnosed with MS each year. For many people, this seems like a death sentence. I am writing this book to provide encouragement for these unfortunate people—and for their loved ones, friends, and caregivers as well. My belief is that if a person lives with a positive attitude, there is hope for a worthwhile life in spite of an MS diagnosis. My goal is to be an example of this theory by sharing my hands-on experiences and the choices I've made. I would like to help ease the anguish resulting from fear of the unknown.

CHAPTER 1

Who is Vickie? Life up to MS

Let me introduce myself. My name is Vickie (Long, Shortley) Berwaldt. Now, does God have a sense of humor or what? For those who know me, this name is well suited (quirky and strangely unique).

Now that you have taken a few minutes to laugh at my expense (poor me), I'd like to share my story of multiple sclerosis and how this complicated disease has impacted my life and relationships throughout the years. *Sooooooo*, find yourself a comfortable chair, grab a cup of coffee, adjust your glasses, and begin to read a story that will hopefully make you laugh—maybe cause a tear or two—but ultimately inform you that there is...*"Life after MS."* R E A L L Y!

I was born August 14, 1945 (VJ day). My parents were either very clever, or my mother had been very heavily drugged. Why, you ask? They chose to name me Vickie Joan Long. Yes, on that very day, the skies of New York City were filled with tons of confetti in celebration of (Vickie's birth?)...VJ day. The United States' victory over Japan—joyously celebrated.

Minneapolis, Minnesota (well known for its ten thousand lakes, mosquitoes, and snow), is my place of birth. I own a T-shirt that says, "Made in America...with Norwegian parts." For me, this is a very accurate description of my heritage. Unfortunately, "Can you speak Norwegian?" are the only words I can say in Norwegian. Clearly, I'd be in sad shape at a Norwegian restaurant with a non-English speaking waitress. If nothing else, I could probably get some lefsa and lutefisk. *Uff-da!*

Throughout this book you're going to see the word *Uff-da* many times. You'll not find this word in the dictionary. This is Norwegian slang used when something bad happens or when you've incorrectly said something. For me, the best description I can share is when I watched *Schindler's List*. The person sitting in front of me must have wondered what it meant because I said it at least fifty times (watching the brutality of children and adults).

I must be very honest and say that my childhood was not the typical *Father Knows Best* household. Unfortunately, my father fought the addiction of alcohol, and I'm sorry to say he lost the battle more often than not. My mother, eighteen years his junior, struggled for years trying to help him. Because of Dad's addiction, my brother and I were witness to several years of turmoil and stressful situations.

When my mother passed away (1976), I was very honest with my father and told him that I didn't know how Mom could have stayed with him as long as she did. I told him I didn't think that I could ever have been married to him for so many years. He knew, however, that my brother and I had forgiven him and also knew that we didn't like everything he had done throughout our past. Despite life, however, we loved our father, and he knew that.

I lived in Minnesota until I was twenty-one, when I married a young man named Paul Shortley. We began married life in East Pittsburgh, Pennsylvania. I'll never forget the comment (made by a guest in our wedding reception line) regarding where we'd be living. When I told her we'd be living in the Pittsburgh area, she remarked, "Oh that's too bad." You can only try to imagine what was going through my thoughts.

Yes, we left Minnesota the day after our wedding in September 1966 and never returned to live in Minneapolis ever again. Paul had recently graduated from the University of Minnesota and was hired by Westinghouse Corporation. This was the reason we left Minnesota.

At times I think back and say, "Wow!" I actually agreed to leave my family and friends and begin married life in a state I had never been in before and didn't know one person there? As the song says, "The things we do for love."

No longer Miss Long, I became Mrs. Shortley. Please, don't deny it; I can hear you laughing out loud. Don't worry, everyone has laughed about this, and they still do. At one of my high school reunions, a friend read my name tag and said, "You've got to be kidding." I said, "No, it's true. It's something, I thought, that could have only happened to me."

I was a *F A I R L Y* typical child—not the overachiever, yet holding a grade point average that allowed my acceptance to the University of Minnesota, a proud and happy experience.

My education began at Lindale, Irving, and Lake Harriet elementary schools; Southwest high school, class of '63 (go Indians—purple/white); as I mentioned, the University of Minnesota (two years) and the Minnesota School of Business. It's fairly obvious that my career choice was not to become a dentist.

With this background, I became secretary to the parts-department manager at Roger's Hydraulic in Minnetonka, Minnesota. Yes, the home of Tonka Toys. Having gotten settled down (in Pittsburgh Steelers country), I worked at the Boyce-campus Community College as secretary to the director of admissions, Mr. McHugh (a good Norwegian name, don't you think? Uff-da!).

Throughout my life, way tooooooo many funny experiences have filled my days. Speaking of humor, I have often been told that I easily make people laugh, that I am funny. I simply say, "Really?" I then tell them that most often, what I say is not pre-planned or scripted. The words just flow out of my mouth. That's the way God made me—beware!

Printed on one of my favorite T-shirts is: "I laughed so hard, that the tears ran down my leg." Please be prepared to read about many of my strangely humorous experiences (involving my MS), creating fond memories indeed. For example, other than myself, I've wondered how many people would laugh after having fallen on top of the scout leader's husband (Chapter 4). Let's just say you had to be there.

Many an unsuspecting person has heard me say that my actual birth name is Vickie Joan *Phyllis Diller* Long. When I hear someone say something, quite often I quickly come up with a humorous reply—a natural instinct. There we go again, another characteristic that God has put into my DNA. For me, it's something like a reaction to an action. Wow! It sounds as if I'm getting scientific. That's not like me at all. My least favorite subject was always science in any shape or form. My grades in this topic were probably Cs or C minuses. Oh well, please don't tell my daughters.

I could easily deviate and write an entire book about the humorous pickles I've gotten myself into. With all the laughing I've done, I'm surprised I still have a voice. In my senior yearbook, for example, printed with my photo you'll read, "Her smile is worth a million, her laughter can't be bought." My German teacher said my laugh reminded him of a dog when its foot gets crunched in the door, and I was once removed (*kicked out of*) student assembly because a teacher heard me laugh. Go figure.

For as long as I can remember, I've enjoyed being involved with other people in a wide variety of ways: as a Luther League youth group treasurer, high school badminton team member, senior choir secretary, Welcome Wagon officer, neighborhood civic secretary, PTA secretary, card club member, church choir member from 1977 'til now, church leadership officer in various capacities, Murder Mystery Dinner Theater actor, MS support group co-founder, etc., etc.

I've thoroughly enjoyed my involvement in each one of these groups. As a result, I have no doubt developed leadership skills, gained greater self-esteem, learned how to play canasta (an absolute must), made many new friends—*and* I have a multitude of fond memories. My problem-solving skills have improved as well as my ability to face challenges with an optimistic point of view.

Other than the fact that I simply enjoy people, I do believe that having left all family and friends behind (in Minnesota) in 1966 and moving to Pennsylvania, and then making the same type of move in 1976 (to Massachusetts), this time leaving many good friends behind, have played a large part in my going from "fairly shy" to "extrovert."

I may not be the sharpest tool in the shed, but it didn't take me any time at all to realize that people were not going to come pounding on our door to say, "We heard you just moved in, so we dropped everything to come say hello." Wasn't going to happen. *Soooo* it was time for me to get involved somehow and make friends.

Joining a church and Welcome Wagon, and getting a job— each opened many opportunities for making friends and acquaintances. These were things that made me feel more at home in Pennsylvania (ten years) and Massachusetts (thirty-six years). Members of both churches, thankfully, quickly became our church family.

As I think back to my high school graduation (some say hearken back), I clearly remember wondering where I would be and what I would be doing in ten years. I did know that I would be attending the University of Minnesota even though I hadn't yet decided upon a major. However, never in a million years (as they say), did I imagine Vickie Long *Shortley* (married, mother of two) living in East Pittsburgh, Pennsylvania. Like most teenagers, healthy and vibrant, I had never given thought to living life with (what could be) a life-altering disease. As a new graduate, I was about to embark on the "real world." For me this meant dealing with new opportunities and challenges and going with the flow.

CHAPTER 2

First Symptoms: My Reaction/Reaction of Family

The question "Vickie, when do you think your MS began?" has often been asked of me. As I look back, I tell them about a reoccurring symptom I experienced three times, between ages fifteen and nineteen.

Before I go into any detail, I would like to reassure you that I have come to know that there is no *one* symptom that causes MS. I find it necessary to tell you this so that people won't self-diagnose themselves needlessly (causing turmoil and fear of the unknown).

Now, getting back to my explanation of early symptoms: Finding myself in the midst of very stressful and emotional situations, i.e., watching a burning building in Iowa, my insecurity and jealousy of my mother's date, standing in front of my father's apartment door knowing that once again he was drunk, caused my body to tremble and shake uncontrollably. These were my first neurological reactions to extreme stress (visible signs of more to come—the MS diagnosis). Because these symptoms were so few and far between, I never really took them seriously. Consequently, my parents knew nothing about them.

June 1967 is when I began to experience serious symptoms that did not go unnoticed. It was also the summer my mother made her very first trip to Pennsylvania. I was soooo very excited (happy stress) about her visit, as anxious as a child waiting for Santa Claus and his gifts. I knew Mom would be seeing our first apartment and how I had decorated it, etc. (it's a female thing).

After she arrived, all I needed to say to her was, "I have a small numb spot on my upper left arm." Big mistake! My thoughts were that it was just a bug bite; end of conversation. Oh contraire. Mom proposed an ultimatum: "If you're not going to call a doctor for a checkup, I will!"

I will? Who on earth was this woman from Minneapolis going to call? OK, OK, OK, she made her point. I paid a visit to our family doctor, and this is where my unwelcome saga began.

At this point, my story is very similar to hundreds of misdiagnosed patients. My doctor's first suggestion was: "Have your husband massage the back of your shoulder. A pinched nerve or tight muscles could be the cause of your numb spot." Calling the very same clinic two months later, I made an appointment with a younger doctor. No, he wasn't exactly a Doogie Howser, but his recent training (up-to-date neurology) prompted him to suggest that I schedule a visit with a neurologist. You see, he must have suspected MS and was sensitive enough not to suggest it to me (*causing fear of the unknown*).

Letting my fingers do the walking, I randomly chose a neurologist close to home. This man's name was Dr. M, and at the end of seven years, I referred to him as Dr. Mickey Mouse and would not refer him to my worst enemy. Wow! Why on earth would I say this? As I try to explain our seven-year (doctor-patient) relationship, I have no doubt you will completely understand his name change. Trust me, I did not make the change to protect the innocent. He was by no means innocent. I can only hope your choice of neurologist ends on a more positive note.

August '67 was my first encounter with Dr. M. After he completed his normal exam (checking eyes, strength, range of motion, balance, etc.), we talked briefly at his desk. An important question he asked was, "Do you have numbness in any part of your body other than your upper left arm?" My answer was "No."

As we continued to talk, I thought it very strange when this man said to me, "Don't do what my wife and I did. We waited too long to start a family. It's good to start a family when you're young." I thought, "What does this have to do with the price of tea in China?" Are you sensing a weird pattern unfolding? Believe me, there's a lot more.

December came, as did the numbness—in both feet and continuing up both legs to my waist. At this point, Dr. M reserved a room for me at the lovely McKeesport hospital. Picture this: a cemetery outside my window and a US Steel mill just across the street. When the train came by, I seriously thought it was coming down the hallway and into my room—really. Uff-da!

After trying every test known to man (to find the cause of the numbness), Dr. M's last procedure was a spinal tap. (In the mid-60s, the MRI did not exist; I'm not sure that it was even on the drawing board.) After the spinal tap, no one told me to lie flat; the doctor must have assumed the nurse told me to lie flat, and the nurse must have assumed the doctor told me to lie flat. Guess what? For the remainder of the day, I sat in an upright position. This is a very clear example of why you should never make assumptions about any professional person—not even doctors.

As my husband left that evening, I mentioned that I felt a headache coming on. By the next morning, the headache became so severe that I nearly wished I were dead. Sad to say, I couldn't have cared less about my husband, my parents, or anyone. I just wanted the horror of the pain to go away.

And now for Dr. M. Three days after the spinal tap, Dr. M came into my room and said something that tempted me to say, "Are you out of your mind?" He looked at me and said, "Don't you wear makeup in the hospital?" I thought, you've got to be joking. I felt like saying, "Oh yes, even though I wish I were dead, putting on makeup is at the top of my priority list—for sure."

Being young and respecting my elders is probably why I bit my tongue and didn't tell him to drop dead. I can only assume that he was using his bedside humor to cheer me up. He failed.

After a week of intravenous ACTH (Acthar), all of the numbness went away. At this point, Dr. M told me that I had neuritis (inflammation of the nervous system) and said that I could go home. I thought it very strange that he never told me to make a follow-up appointment. I was on my own at this point. This again was an example of his weird medical ethic.

Exactly one year later, I mentioned to a coworker that I was experiencing something very strange with my right eye. I told her that I could see things on my left and right (peripheral vision), but could see nothing in front of me.

Not being a Florence Nightingale, I thought this was a by-product of my horrific cold or a side effect of my neuritis. At this point, Dr. M sent me to an eye specialist. This man told me that I was experiencing optic neuritis and prescribed ACTH in pill form. Once again, this medication worked perfectly for me. My vision problem vanished, and I could see clearly. Still, no one had mentioned the words "multiple sclerosis." *Sooooooo*, my neuritis must be acting up, was what I thought.

Proud as I could be, I gave birth to two lovely daughters (Lynn Marie—1970) and (Dawn Michelle—1975). I can tell you now that I never did get the Mother of the Year award. In my own defense, however, the hospital never did give me a manual on how to raise children. On the other hand, the telephone company named me to their Customer of the Month Club. Everyone enjoys recognition and awards for good deeds, but the only requirement was daily long-distance phone calls to Minnesota (mom, mother-in-law, and my brother's wife Linda—each being experienced mothers).

The building of our very first home and the birth of our daughters filled me with happy excitement. My reason for mentioning these two occasions is that I have come to the conclusion that the bad type of stress and the happy-excitement type are often equally harmful for me. At this time, putting a damper on things, Dr. M struck once more.

Without the use of e-mail or Facebook, I often wrote to many family and friends in Minnesota. Doing so, I noticed that my handwriting was slower than usual and a bit awkward. This prompted yet another visit with Dr. M. I told him about Lynn (our first daughter). Once again, Dr. M's weird ethics shouted loud and clear.

Out of nowhere, he said to me, "Oftentimes, husbands will leave women with conditions like you have." A few sentences later, the man who had once prompted my husband and me to start a family said, "If I were you, I'd go home and talk to your husband about not having any more children."

Forty-plus years have erased my memory of our specific conversation at that point. However, without having been given any explanation for these comments, I can only imagine that my mind must have been whirling and numbed.

As I do in most cases, I gave Dr. M the benefit of the doubt and thought about seeing him again. The year was 1972, a frightening time for me. The phrase "fear of the unknown" sums it up rather well.

I was pushing Lynn in the grocery cart when without warning, I knew that I was going to have a bowel movement, but I couldn't do anything to stop it. Thankful that I was wearing dark pants, I picked Lynn up and left the filled cart in the middle of the aisle. I drove home, put Lynn into the playpen, then quickly took a shower. Nobody knew what had happened, but I was extremely embarrassed.

My husband made the phone call to Dr. M, telling him of my situation. Dr. M told my husband that I should go back to the hospital for more testing. At that moment my husband said, "Since Vickie saw you last, we've moved. Can she go to the Greensburg hospital instead of McKeesport?" The first thing that came out of that man's mouth was, "Why? Doesn't she like the food at McKeesport hospital?" This was the final straw for me. I never wanted to see or talk to him again—*ever!*

The phrase "as one door closes, another door is opened" was at work in my life. My friend Eileen, a nurse at the Greensburg Hospital, recommended an on-staff neurologist whom I should see. Referrals are great. I learned (after my first appointment) that this doctor had served on the National MS Society's board of trustees for many years. No more poor bedside manner for me. I thanked God.

Within fifteen minutes of hearing the explanation of my neuritis symptoms (beginning at age fifteen), Dr. Rosen said, "Vickie, you have multiple sclerosis, and your doctor must have known because he was treating you for it." Needless to say, a diagnosis with a sting to it. For reasons of his own, Dr. M had chosen not to tell me.

Tearful, frightened, emotional, horrified? My first reaction to this correct diagnosis included none of these feelings. You see, I knew almost nothing about MS. Soooooo, my lack of knowledge enabled me to seem fearless. I actually knew only one person with this disease, an older lady from church. Not being totally aware of this woman's medical history, I was really ignorant of how my life could change.

At the time of my correct diagnosis by Dr. Rosen, I was actually more curious than stressfully anxious, making life less complicated for me and my family at the time. My lack of MS knowledge reminds me of the phrase "ignorance is bliss."

I have no doubt that the confirmation of multiple sclerosis was not what my husband or parents wanted to hear. I know that when I gave her this news by telephone, Mom must have cried after we hung up. For my benefit, however, I received positive reactions and support from both family and friends. Fear of the unknown was no longer a part of my life, as I did research to learn more about the disease that had caught me off guard.

Finally, my family and I knew what I was dealing with. Now I (we) could make some adjustments. Specifically for me, no more soaking in a hot bathtub, no getting overheated or too tired, etc., etc. It was my desire to live a happy life regardless of the changes and disappointments that may occur. My choice has always been to be an optimist because being a pessimist (I think) is a waste of my time—and it's not fun. And, oh yes, I am also realistic. The unexpected does happen; it's called life.

My introduction to cortisone (two injections per day) was a prescription by Dr. Rosen. My husband conveniently gave them to me at home. The reason for using cortisone was to slow down the progression of further symptoms. Other than the two pinches per day (needles, mind you), I was truly unaware of the bizarre side effects that were about to briefly turn my life upside down.

Throughout my history of MS, I've been told most people's cortisone side effects are excess weight gain and a bloated face. I, on the other hand, have never had this happen. My reaction to cortisone has been quite the opposite.

With instructions of two weeks for injections, I became alarmed after the eighth day. I had come to realize that (number one) at night; I would sleep for three hours and wake up refreshed as though I had slept for eight hours. Having woken up refreshed (number two), while my family was sleeping soundly, I would wash floors, iron clothes, write letters, or want to do whatever task came to mind. Instead of gaining weight (number three), I quickly lost pounds (I wasn't overweight).

Other than the non-sleeping issue, you may be wondering why I complain about losing weight and accomplishing every task on my to-do list. Just about any woman I know would be thrilled to achieve these things. I, on the other hand, gradually realized that I was sacrificing my sanity.

Unable to contact my doctor, I informed my husband I was no longer going to continue these shots. Whether it is a simple aspirin or flu shot, I adamantly refused to take any kind of medicine. That very Sunday, I went to my bedroom to take a nap (sleep deprivation). After waking up I went into the kitchen and asked my husband if he had heard any noise coming from our bedroom. You see, I had fallen into such a deep sleep that my nightmare had convinced me I was thrashing around attempting to hurt myself.

An unexpectedly bizarre issue came about as a result of my sudden weight loss. In my Thursday morning bowling group, a woman (supposedly my friend) was actually jealous (and showed it) because of my weight loss. In my own mind (not out loud), I couldn't help but wonder how she would enjoy an incurable disease enabling her to lose weight. I do believe she would change her mind in a heartbeat.

My memory, unfortunately, does not recall the exact details of my doctor's solution to this problem. I am happy to report that my bizarre side effects were resolved. Then I was on my own if I wanted to lose a pound or two. Weight Watchers, perhaps.

CHAPTER 3

Marriage: what does Husband Think? is He Supportive?

Can my relationship survive MS? This was the topic of an article I read, and the answer was YES! Your relationship may not only survive, but may actually strengthen as a couple unites to fight a common enemy.

When couples understand how the disease may affect their relationship, learn how to cope with the added stress it may bring, and put preventive measures into place, the outcome is (more often than not) positive.

When people are diagnosed, fear of being abandoned by their partners and worry of becoming a burden are natural concerns. Disaster may occur if these concerns are acted upon rather than voiced. Rather than thinking, "I was certain he would leave me," express your concerns and avoid anxiety.

Among the challenges is that of finding harmony and fulfillment in your relationship. These require serious planning and effort (by both partners) when MS is involved. Thinking outside the box works wonders. Working in the kitchen (using adaptable equipment), the laundry room, the nursery—and the bedroom. An occupational therapist is trained to assess your needs and will enable you to complete tasks with less effort. Issues of intimacy, on the other hand, require the expertise of a professional sex therapist.

Couples are urged to remain open to role changes. Those who succeed in negotiating the demands of MS are well aware that symptom flare-ups and exacerbations may necessitate temporary role changes. Healthy partners often shift roles the most. Caregivers, however, should not sacrifice their own needs and desires to the point of losing themselves in their spouses' illness. The relationship may die when this happens. Do your very best to maintain a healthy balance (of roles) in order to avoid disaster.

From my point of view, role changes required certain agreements between partners. A willingness to step in when needed and lend a helping hand—carrying groceries in from the car, putting the third load of laundry into the washer and dryer, picking up pizza for dinner so I could avoid our hot kitchen, finishing vacuuming when I got to the point of falling down, etc., etc.

If it had been my husband (diagnosed with MS), I would have gladly helped in similar ways. When we got married, I remember saying words such as "I promise," "in sickness and in health," "for better or worse," "till death do us part..." and then I kissed the groom.

Communicate, communicate, and communicate! To maintain a healthy, loving relationship, communication is of utmost importance. This is even more important when MS enters the picture. If you keep your emotions and feelings inside, issues of misunderstanding and assumption (and depression) can ruin even the best of relationships. Be honest with each other and talk things through.

My first husband, Paul, was very supportive. "In sickness and in health" are vows that he took seriously. No matter what, he went (I thought) far and above the call of duty. Unfortunately, I have met some couples (male and female MSers) with partners who have forgotten the "and in sickness" clause.

Bob, my current husband of almost four years, is supportive beyond belief. You see, he was diagnosed with MS several years ago. We have no need to explain our temporary lack of energy, or weakness, or awkward balance, or slurred speech, or not wanting to sit in the hot sun etc., etc. Each of us has experienced some of these symptoms at one time or another and realizes the consequences of some of them.

From time to time Bob and I have told family and friends, "You will never find two MS people experiencing the exact same symptom at the very same time." This disease is not like the measles: first this happens, then that happens, then this will happen, and finally, this will happen to you, and your measles are gone.

We support and encourage each other, often thinking outside the box and putting our creative juices to work.

We've learned ways in which MS people and their partners can transform and improve their quality of life.

In an effort to maintain healthy relationships within your immediate family, you can make specific choices to accomplish your goals. With certain modifications (as needed), traveling is said to be good for the soul and can improve your outlook on life. Trips can also get your family away from their daily routines. Traveling can give each of you space away from your ongoing MS issues (a change of scenery). I will repeat my suggestion once again: "There is life after MS." REALLY!

Pioneer Valley MS Support Group was legally incorporated (1979) by Bob, three other MSers and me, and Sister Mary Dennis, an MS office manager (also diagnosed with MS). As with other support groups, a variety of guest speakers spoke to us (during our monthly meetings) in the areas of MS research updates, appropriate exercise techniques, yoga, availability of Lifeline (an emergency call device), family life (very important for children), intimacy and sexuality issues, travel, and information etc. etc.

Our group also learned that the National Multiple Sclerosis Society is an excellent source of age-appropriate reading materials—books, pamphlets, audio/visual materials, etc.—describing this complicated disease in detail. Marriage seminars were always well attended, as were research updates led by a panel of doctors at various seminars or via teleconferencing.

Having become a widow (2002), marrying Bob (2008) is one of the best decisions I've ever made. I'll go into further detail about Bob in Chapter 10—good stuff, I promise. Actually, I seriously believe God had our futures on the back burner from the time we first met.

CHAPTER 4

Bearing Children and Raising Them—How Is This Possible?

"Does this mean that I can't have children?" Women of child bearing age diagnosed with MS most often have this specific question for their neurologist. In my case, my first child arrived during the neuritis phase of my MS (good old Dr. M's diagnosis). Did I say good? Scratch that.

I was completely unaware of my MS when our first daughter (Lynn) was born on May 15, 1970—8 lb. 2 oz., 20 inches tall. As first-time parents, my husband and I were happy beyond belief. It was then that we entered a new phase in life, parenthood.

Other than fatigue from sleepless nights, my side effects were few (both daughters). I clearly remember, however, the morning we brought Lynn home from the hospital. Picture this: I was comfortable in my bed, Lynn was in her crib, and my husband was getting ready to return to the office. Before he left, however, he asked me a question. I was unable to speak, to make a reply. Why? I have never been able to cry and talk at the same time. I resorted to writing notes. You see, unbeknownst to me, I was experiencing the "afterbirth blues." One of my greatest concerns was, "Will I be as good a mother as my mom was?" You guessed it: my emotions had kicked into severe overdrive.

By the way, did I mention falling asleep (2:00 a.m.) while using my electric typewriter? (Lynn was three days old). The first part of my letter was perfectly fine, bragging to family about our new arrival. The last paragraph, however, made absolutely no sense whatsoever. In fact, it resembled a foreign language of unknown origin. As I dozed off, you see, my hands remained on top of the keyboard—the electric keyboard. Details, no doubt, aren't necessary.

While on the topic of sleep (or lack thereof), I must tell you of another bizarre "new-mom-Vickie" episode. While eating breakfast (Lynn's fourth day home), my husband said to me, "Do you remember what you were doing to me last night?"

I said, "Good grief, what do you mean? What I was doing to you?"

He proceeded to say, "You were fondling me and treating me like the baby."

I blurted out, "What on earth do you mean?" You see, I had fallen into a very deep sleep and a frightening nightmare. I was convinced that Lynn was somewhere in our bed and suffocating. I insisted (in no uncertain terms) that he wake up and help me find her. It's a wonder he could even function at work the next day. Uff-da!

Before my husband and I ever thought of a second child, I thanked God I was able to raise Lynn just like any other healthy mother. Other than a few minor neuritis episodes (and going from four hours of sleep per night to a heavenly seven hours), there was never the hint of a potentially cruel disease coming my way.

August 1974 was when I paid Dr. Rosen a routine annual visit. He was eager to tell me of a new medication, Imuran, he wanted me to start taking. The purpose of this drug was to slow the progression of symptoms (such as the numbness I experienced). However, because this drug was a form of poison, I could not become pregnant while taking it.

Needless to say, when I told him that I was five months pregnant, he congratulated me and suggested I have a tubal legation the day after delivery. With no complications, Dawn was born on January 3, 1975, and my tubes were tied the next day.

As may be the case, neurologists may differ in their opinions regarding pregnancy and MS. For your peace of mind, I would suggest that you consult with more than one doctor. A serious decision such as this requires as much information as you can gather. Dr. Rosen felt that my pregnancy would not be compromised because of multiple sclerosis. Thankfully, he was correct.

From my own experience, I would venture to say that for any family with an MS parent, thinking outside the box (as I said before) and being creative are necessary components in day-to-day living. Knowing that this disease is extremely complicated and unpredictable, affecting every person differently, we each create our own ways of adapting to change. Hopefully this is done in productive and healthy ways.

My reasoning reminds me often that necessity is the mother of invention, such as making an arm sling using a hand towel and duct tape. Oh yes, I did this until I got the real thing. And helping my daughters with art projects using my paper cutter—not being able to handle scissors.

As my mobility, coordination, and strength gradually decreased, I was forced to achieve my goals by unusual methods. My way of doing certain tasks has often appeared to be oddly DIFFERENT, but I've eventually accomplished the results as planned. This method of adapting has helped me as a wife, mother, committee member, friend, and productive and happy person. I've often said that MS has made me a better person. I've used brain cells I didn't know existed—ho ho ho.

How and when you decide to communicate about MS with your children is really each parent's choice. Lynn, our oldest daughter, was four and a half when Dawn was born. Our decision to not tell Lynn about my diagnosis was probably due to the fact I wasn't really showing many obvious symptoms. At this time, we felt that a family discussion explaining MS wasn't necessary. However, when Dawn was four, my friend (her daycare teacher) asked to talk to my husband and me. I couldn't imagine why a parent-teacher conference was necessary for a four-year-old.

Our parent-teacher discussion primarily focused on Dawn's need for attention. The teacher told us that Dawn tended to forget instructions, which required her teacher to sit with her and explain the task again. I was totally at a loss to suggest why she would do that. I reassured my friend that at home, Lynn and Dawn were treated equally—no favoritism or special treatment given to either one.

Two months had gone by when Dawn's kindergarten teacher requested that I make an appointment to talk with her. She told me that Dawn had taken some finger paint (from her easel) and proceeded to paint on her desk. After I told this woman about Dawn's peculiar behavior at daycare, she made a very good suggestion. She referred us to the Osborne clinic. This was a local group of child psychologists whom we hoped would be able to get to the bottom of Dawn's unusual behavior.

Before I took Dawn to the clinic, one of the doctors on staff interviewed my husband and me. We were very impressed by how thorough his questions were. While we were sharing information about Dawn, he asked us whether or not she was a planned pregnancy and whether or not we had forced her to potty train too early, etc. Needless to say, the clinic had more than enough information about Dawn to prepare for her first appointment.

By the end of session four, the psychologist explained that Dawn said, more than once, she thought I was going to die (having watched me fall or walk awkwardly). He recommended that we plan family talks around our table to share our feelings and concerns about my illness. As concerned parents, our goal was to explain (on their level), and to reassure them that I wasn't going to die because of my multiple sclerosis.

When considering your decision to talk to your children about MS, there are a variety of issues to think about. It has been said that kids tend to worry when they know that something's up, even if Mom or Dad has no visible symptoms.

As a parent you may struggle with how to talk to your children about MS and the ways it may affect your family. You may be thinking: How much should I tell my children about MS? Will talking about it make it more confusing, frightening, or burdensome for them and me?

It is common for parents to want to protect their children by hiding painful issues. However, it has been said that children are far less fragile than we think. Many believe that open and honest communication is valuable and important. Discovering comfortable ways to talk about MS can be an important step in that process.

Improving or maintaining family functioning is key to helping you and your children adapt to life with MS. Today, in 2012, the National MS Society has several age-appropriate resources (books, videos etc.) available that clearly and easily describe the disease and possible effects to people and their families. These resources help immensely to dismiss their fear of the unknown.

In an age-appropriate way, some parents choose to answer all questions about their MS (with their children), directly and honestly. As the children get older, parents adjust the information accordingly. Some parents choose to say little or nothing about the disease. Each parent deals with this situation as he or she feels is best for the family.

Some MS parents consider their children to be more considerate, gentle, and compassionate as a result of living with an MS parent. They tend to be unafraid of people who are different. For example, children will talk with a neighbor (sitting in a wheelchair) and see nothing unusual. They see only the person they can describe their Christmas gifts to. I am proud to say that both Lynn and Dawn exhibit these characteristics and will hopefully pass this on to my grandchildren.

I'm very thankful to have been able to be a f a i r l y active mom: pre-school helper, Vacation Bible School director, chauffeur to dance classes and doctors appointments, soccer games, school shopping, sleepovers, Girl Scout events, etc. etc. By the way, did I tell you I fell on top of the troop leader's husband?

This poor unsuspecting man offered to carry me (piggyback) up two flights of stairs to Dawn's scout meeting. At the top of our ascent, this guy was doomed. You see, as I got into a standing position, he made a bad assumption—she's safe and stable. Oh contraire. We both fell forward, and I plopped on top of him. With no harm done, we simply laughed and laughed some more. Of God's many gifts to me, I am especially thankful for a healthy sense of humor and for people who understand it.

This chapter deals with how it was possible for me to raise children while living with MS. Well, as the song says, "With a little help from my friends...husband...and family, etc." There were times that I did it with A LOT of help from them—for sure. As I've said so many times, God has blessed me in many ways throughout my life. Motherhood is just one of the examples I'm grateful for, and I am especially thankful to those who have helped me (in so many ways) along the way.

I give an extreme amount of credit to both Lynn and Dawn for all they've done, throughout their lives, to help me achieve daily tasks such as getting dressed sometimes (with buttons and zippers), pulling me out of the bathtub (once) because of my lack of strength, putting on shoes and socks, going into the grocery store (for one item) while I waited in the car, helping me onto my exercise table, etc.

That reminds me of the day I was strapped onto the exercise table and Lynn got a call from a girlfriend. During their conversation, I heard Lynn say, "Just a minute. I have to take my mom off the table." I thought this poor girl must have been wondering, why is her mother on the table?

Lynn and Dawn have been put into precarious situations as a result of helping me. I clearly remember the day Lynn drove my van as I sat in my manual wheelchair behind her. Just having come off a certain medication, I didn't realize my strength was not up to par. Soooooo, as Lynn accelerated from a stop sign, I proceeded to let go of the safety strap. I fell on my back and slid to the rear of the van. What a flattering sight: legs up in the air, etc.

Needless to say, Lynn was horrified and asked if I was all right. As I tried to reassure her that I was fine, I couldn't stop laughing my head off. This experience just struck me as terribly funny. I told her to go into the nearby school parking lot and ask for help. Can you imagine her asking someone to help pick her mother up off the van floor? I wondered if the man thought I might have alcohol on my breath. Oh well.

I have no doubt that from time to time, both girls may have thought I expected too much from them. In the back of their minds, they knew that none of their girlfriends' mothers had ever asked them to do things that they did for me. Without their help, however, there are many tasks I would not have been able to do by myself.

Joyce, my church's office manager, complimented me years ago because Lynn and Dawn were both such capable and responsible young girls (having been trained to do many things for me). I was very pleased by her comment and was a very proud mother indeed.

As I was driving one day with both girls in the backseat, we saw a young man using Canadian crutches awkwardly crossing the street. I reminded the girls of how grateful we should be not to be living with that disability. I probably said, "There but for the grace of God go I." This is a phrase I have said many times because I do know that my circumstances could be so much worse than they are.

"Mother, do you have to talk to everyone?" Even now, at ages 42 and 38, Lynn and Dawn continue to ask me this question. This character trait fits me to a T. Yes, I do consider myself to be a friendly and congenial person. I believe the saying goes: A stranger is just a friend I haven't met yet. Quite often I say that I may have been shy at one time, but because it was soooo long ago, I really don't remember.

Having said all this, other than the adaptations I've had to make, parenthood has been just as challenging for me as it has been for all parents. And just as rewarding. I thank God for trusting me to become a parent.

CHAPTER 5

How Faith Came into the Picture—What It Meant for Me

About fifteen years ago, I was asked to write a brief article in our church newsletter on the subject of "My Faith." Five other members were asked to do the same.

To be very honest with you, I don't remember everything I wrote. I didn't keep the article. However, I distinctly remember saying that I would describe my faith as a work in progress. Today, if I were asked to write on the same topic, I'd probably say the very same thing. I believe my faith continues to be a work in progress. There is still so much more for me to learn and experience in God's ministry. The notion that you can't teach an old dog new tricks is certainly not true in my opinion.

Having been very young at the time of my diagnosis, I did not fully understand God's plan for my life, nor did I fully trust in his promise to guide me through tough challenges. Consequently, I relied on my own strengths, asking myself, "Why did this happen to me?"

A combination of events led me to understand my circumstances and reminded me that God's with me each step of the way. I've listened carefully to the message of pastors' sermons (how they've pertained to my life). I've learned much from Bible studies and discussion groups. Church choirs have enabled me to hear God's word within the hymns. I've gone on mission trips to South Carolina. One of the best teaching tools for me has been to OBSERVE and LISTEN to Christians—they not only "talk the talk," but they genuinely "walk the walk."

I believe that hope is a short but powerful word. Dealing with the uncertainties of MS complications, often I had doubts and very little room for thoughts of a future with hope. Inviting God into my life and believing his word have taught me to have not fear but hope—for a better life through Jesus Christ.

I invited God into my life in 1968 when I found that I was lost without him. I asked forgiveness for my wrongs and then asked Jesus Christ to come into my heart and be my lord and savior. I want to live for him. I heard the truth, and the truth set me free. This "truth set me free" comment could be thought of as corny, but it is true.

Many of the people reading this are searching for hope. In some way, I want to show them the salvation message that will convey the fact Jesus died for our sins. Ten important words to remember are: "I can do all things through Christ, who strengthens me."

Speaking of the word *hope*: While growing up, as I wrote about earlier, I learned an awesome lesson from my mother. Her example spoke volumes. For the most part, Mom faced very difficult challenges: she lost the battle of trying to help my alcoholic father; she was physically and verbally abused; she supported and raised my brother and me, etc. As I mentioned earlier, during these difficult times, I never saw her walking around with a placard declaring, "I've lived a very rough life, and I've succeeded (and you can too)." From mere observation, I learned a lesson on how to make the best of my situation(s) knowing that with God's help, I can make a difference resulting in hope for my future.

I am a part of the Stephen's Ministry program at my current church, and we often share in continuing-study topics. I particularly remember talking about the word *salt*, which is mentioned three times in the Bible. Before we were told this fact, we were asked to give our reasons for using salt when we cook and eat. Without a doubt, everyone agreed that salt improves and enhances the flavor of most foods. Salt seems to give it a little pizzazz. It is a beneficial seasoning, enriching flavors.

I have no doubt that you're probably wondering how the discussion of salt could have anything to do with my faith (remember, I've admitted to being peculiar). At the end of our continuing study on salt, I came to a conclusion that puts my words into action.

It is my belief that you and I are asked to be the salt: to think about WHAT TO DO WITH WHO WE ARE. That is, how can we enrich the lives of others, enhance it, and let others see God in us—how we "walk the walk." I guess you could say that my life and faith have been overly salted by others. Contrary to what doctors may think about the health dangers of excess salt, its biblical context—enriching others—is (as Martha Stewart would say) "a good thing."

Computers conjure up mixed emotions for me. On the one hand, I've advanced from feelings of intimidation (didn't even want to turn it on) to the point of turning it on early in the day to check e-mails, etc. Yes, there have been several times, I must admit, that frustration would have easily prompted me to throw it out a window. The only reason it's still on my desk is that I lack the strength to pick it up and toss it.

My reason for telling you my thoughts on computers is that I truly admire their capabilities, their unlimited resources, their ability to save time in our busy schedules, etc. I especially enjoy receiving e-mails (inspirational, educational, and humorous).

At this point, I'm going to share an e-mail message that expresses my Christian beliefs rather well. I cannot quote its source, but the subject line reads: Thanks for being my friend.

When you feel like you're drowning in life, don't worry—your Life guard walks on water.

When I say that I am a Christian, I am not shouting that I am clean living.

I'm whispering I was lost, but now I'm found and forgiven.

When I say I am Christian, I'm not trying to be strong,

I'm confessing that I stumble and need Christ to be my guide.

When I say I am Christian, I'm not bragging of success.

I'm admitting I have failed and need God to clean my mess.

When I say I am a Christian, I'm not claiming to be perfect.

My flaws are far too visible, but God believes I'm worth it.

When I say I am a Christian, I still feel the sting of pain.

I have my share of heartaches, so I call upon his name.

When I say I am a Christian, I'm not holier than thou.

I'm just a simple sinner who received God's grace.

Be Blessed, Be a Blessing

Along with all I've shared, I will repeat the fact that I still refer to my faith as a work in progress. God is not done with me yet—no way. I am assured that he will be at my side to guide me, strengthen me, and care for me as I face the unexpected challenges that may come my way.

CHAPTER 6

Symptoms Worsen—Bee Therapy

This chapter comes with a warning: everything you're about to read pertains only to me. My ups and downs, my good days and bad days, my exacerbations and depressions, etc., etc. By no means should you think that you or your loved ones will experience the exact same symptoms as mine. MS continues to be an unsolved mystery, and I pray that one day, MS will mean "Mystery Solved."

As I've suggested in earlier chapters, multiple sclerosis has a varied and unpredictable course. It's an individual disease. Therefore, it is not helpful to compare one person to another— the onset and severity of symptoms vary far too much. It has been said that there are few diseases with more potential symptoms than MS.

To be very honest, when I was correctly diagnosed, I had no clue as to the possible symptoms commonly associated with MS: vision; motor skills; coordination and balance; fatigue; sensory, bowel, bladder, sexual, and cognitive symptoms, etc. Accordingly,

I'll share my experiences with certain issues and a variety of treatments that I've used, most often prescribed by my neurologist. Then there was the honeybee venom therapy I volunteered for. I'll be telling you about my three hundred stings (and results) in this chapter.

Yes, my neurologist, Dr. LM, with his good sense of humor (not Dr. M), often said that I could try things—special diets, vitamins, exercises, treatments etc., as long as they caused me no harm. I would say he trusted me to use basic common sense.

The course of my multiple sclerosis began at age fifteen (mentioned in chapter 2), an extremely emotional occurrence that repeated itself at the age of seventeen and again at nineteen. A period of three years followed without noticeable progression of symptoms.

Summer of 1967 came, and with it came a numb spot in my upper left arm. My assumption was that it must be a bug bite (mentioned briefly in chapter 2). After several visits to my family doctor and neurologist, the numbness occurred in both feet, up both legs to my waist. This symptom prompted the doctor (Dr. M) to schedule a hospital visit.

As I have already told you, my exam was very thorough, including a spinal tap and intravenous ATCH medication. It was the spinal fluid that indicated the MS (scar tissue on my spine and brain). The ATCH IVs caused the numbness to vanish. It was my Pennsylvania neurologist (not doctor M) who told me that my category (level) of MS was secondary progressive (a very, very slow decline of functions over a long period of time).

While talking with coworkers (winter of '68), I said that it must have been because of a bad cold that my eyes were doing something strange. Needless to say, they asked me what I meant by a strange. I explained that I couldn't see the person in front of me, but I could see the person beside me.

Following visits to the neurologist and eye specialist, my diagnosis was optic neuritis, and it was treated with ACTH in pill form (my vision was corrected). This experience definitely placed me in the "possible visual symptoms" category.

When describing my early symptoms, I said that my hand-writing had noticeably slowed down quite a bit. Having the ability to take shorthand dictation at work, I knew that something was wrong. Unfortunately I had made an incorrect assumption. I thought this issue must be caused by my neuritis (good old Dr. M). Uff-da! This experience, I would say, now has definitely placed me in the "possible motor symptoms" category.

The highlight of 1970 was the birth of my first daughter, Lynn. Fatigue was no greater for me than for any other new mom (previously mentioned). When describing some of my early MS symptoms, I did tell you about my typewriter episode and my very real nightmare (searching my bed for Lynn). These two examples clearly placed me in the "possible fatigue" category.

At about the same time, I began to notice that my bladder muscle was weakening. This symptom also caused many embarrassing moments. Without mentioning this to my doctor, I simply made the decision to wear a pad to protect my clothing. I was experiencing a new symptom (similar to the bowel issue), and it put me in the "possible incontinence" category.

Enough of my possible category situations. I do believe it's time for a bit of humor, which is something I can easily write about. To be specific, I'm going to tell you about one of my weekend visits with Dawn, Rob, and Jasmine. In particular, I'm going to share a priceless comment made by three-year-old Jasmine (as they say, out of the mouths of babes).

Of course, Jasmine expressed her comment in their bathroom while Dawn was getting me ready for bed. When Dawn was putting on my PJ bottoms, Jasmine asked, "Grandma, why are you wearing diapers?" Without even taking time for a breath, I answered, "Jasmine, these are not diapers. They are called pull-ups."

This was my attempt to associate dignity with the loss of yet another (take it for granted) bodily function.

Joking aside, years later (2009) I made a good, but very difficult, decision as a result of my constant wetness and fear of painful open sores.

After talking with Bob and a urologist, I knew it was time for me to employ good common sense and agree to having a super-pubic catheter inserted into my bladder. I believe that I was reluctant because this process was yet another form of loss, and I knew I'd have to live with it until my last days on earth.

Having adjusted to this lifestyle change, I would jokingly say that one of the worst problems I'm forced to live with is not being able to wear shorts any longer. Actually, when I stop to think about it, that's probably a good thing. The legs don't quite look like they did when I was eighteen.

After being correctly diagnosed (1972) and reading about MS, I knew that my type of MS was the secondary progressive form. That is, as briefly mentioned earlier, a form in which remissions are characterized by gradual deterioration of nerve function, with or without relapses.

Within the same time frame, I noticed lack of sleep often caused double vision when trying to focus. This happened while watching television or reading, etc. In order for me to see one object or word, I had to close one eye. I've dealt with this symptom for a very long time, continuing to this very day.

I have experienced sensory symptoms that have included partial numbness and tingling sensations. I'm thankful that my doctor has prescribed medications that have eliminated these issues.

Through the years, I've noticed that one specific drug may help my friend but does absolutely nothing to help me. Then again, I may benefit from a certain drug, but it does absolutely nothing to help my friend. Just as other MSers are open to their doctors' suggestions of trying a new medication, knowing it will cause me no harm, my thoughts are, Why not give it a try?

My coordination and balance gradually began to change, as did the speed of my walking. I have no doubt that because of not knowing my situation, people made a common assumption: I had too much alcohol.

It was 1976 that I saw a noticeable change in my walking. I attribute this to the fact it was a time of extreme stress. My dear mother died in February, and we sold our home and moved to Massachusetts in December. The problem was that I had never been to this state, nor did I know anybody there.

After I fell a few times, my neurologist suggested I use a cane. From that, I chose to use a four-pronged cane for even better balance. For a good while I felt safe using the four-pronged cane. At this point, however, my doctor suggested I use a walker.

I didn't think, nor would you, that this chapter would leave much room for humor. However, I must tell you about my memorable walker story.

As my walker and I approached a group of people, I couldn't help but notice that one lady looked as though she was about to cry. As I got closer to the group I simply said, "Why bother running? This makes it easier for my husband to catch me." I'd much rather see people smile than see them with tears in their eyes.

I've been known to say, "If I had to focus on my breathing while using my walker, I really don't think I'd be alive to talk about it." You see, quite often I'd use my walker while talking to a friend. More often than not, if I began to laugh, I would have to stop walking. I learned that I had to focus on my balance and concentrate on my walking. Something like not being able to chew gum and walk at the same time?

One of my favorite memories (linking humor with MS) was when I received an invitation to my twentieth high-school reunion. The reunion committee made themselves very clear when they instructed all classmates to write about their life after graduation. The part I liked best is when they specifically told us: "Make your comments interesting."

My electric typewriter was anxiously awaiting my eloquent thoughts. Before I began to follow the committee's instructions, I thought about a seriously important message that I wanted to convey to my former classmates. There were only three classmates who knew I would be sitting in a wheelchair. My thoughts were, I didn't want to travel all the way from Massachusetts to Minnesota to sit in a corner being ignored just because of the wheelchair.

From experience, I have found that many people may want to talk to me. However, because they are afraid they may say the wrong thing, they don't say anything at all. This is a fairly common reaction, unfortunately. I have always enjoyed class re-unions talking—with as many people as I can. Soooooo, I wanted my story to convince classmates that I hadn't changed a bit; I just don't play volleyball or badminton anymore.

Needless to say, I wanted my story to catch people's attention. I am glad to say that my words raised a few eyebrows (for good reasons). Before I begin to tell you what I wrote, however, I must share my eight-year-old daughter's very stern comment. She said, "Mother, you can't say that!" I said to her, "Oh yes I can." You see, there was method to my madness.

Are you ready for this? This is exactly what I wrote: "Just having recently been released from the Western Massachusetts Women's Correctional Institute (for charges of prostitution and theft)..." Well, the committee said to make my comments inter-esting, but they didn't say I had to tell the truth.

After this opening statement, I actually got serious and began to write about life after high school. I was so very glad when many classmates thanked me for making them feel comfortable around me.

I achieved my goal and thoroughly enjoyed sharing thoughts and memories with so many people. In fact, a few classmates said things like: "My wife was just diagnosed," or "My co-worker was recently diagnosed," etc. As a result, we had some worthwhile conversations. I am always very willing to share my thoughts and experiences about MS when asked to do so.

With the help of our insurance, I purchased my first three-wheeled scooter (wheelchair) in 1988. Instead of walking from one end of our house to the other and becoming exhausted, with the help of the scooter I could maneuver our house and still have energy to accomplish things. I must say that I have covered many miles through the years, achieving such things as going on walks, driving up the ramp for choir and up to the stage at our church Murder Mystery theater, and going Christmas shopping at the mall.

One of the most enjoyable memories I have when talking about the scooter is with my grandchildren. Lynn (mother of five-year-old twins) and I took Keera Ann and Brady to the Dairy

Queen (seven blocks away). No cars involved, we walked (they walked). Returning home, my scooter became a train. Yes, I was the engineer, and the twins were my passengers. Keera stood on top of front wheel cover, and Brady stood behind me with his arms around my neck. We had fun. Even Jasmine, now twelve, bummed a ride when she was younger.

Please note this: my intention is not to have you think I consider MS a laughing matter or that I take the easy way out and purposely use humor to mask pain. Humor can do that for people, I understand. However, as my late friend Cecilia Avey told me, "Vickie, if you could write a book the way you talk, it would be a good book." Consequently, as you read this book I'd like you to know that I'm just being honest and telling it as it is. It's about me being me—seasoned with my true sense of humor.

The category of "cognitive symptoms" is one that I have not escaped. These symptoms are described as short-term and long-term memory problems, forgetfulness, and slow word recall. Because I'm no longer twenty-one, I simply refer to these incidents as "senior moments." This observation may be very true, but because of living with MS for so many years, I experience these symptoms more often than I'd like. However, these issues are not a twenty-four seven occurrence, and for that I thank God.

Depression is yet another form of cognitive symptoms, one that I must say I dislike the most. It's a cruel and life-changing experience (for you and those around you) that takes complete control of your thinking, and one's rational thoughts go out the window.

Without invitation or welcome, depression has taken away my appetite, my rational thinking, my self-esteem, my commitment to complete tasks, my desire to laugh and have fun, my wanting to socialize, my desire for intimacy with my husband, etc. Plainly said, it's the pits.

Within my lifetime, I've experienced depression at least four times. While I was mourning the death of my first husband, depression reared its ugly head. Feelings of loss, fear of handling finances, feelings of doubt and guilt, irrational thinking, etc., turned me into someone other than myself—not a very likable person.

Following my last episode, nearly two years ago, I finally put the puzzle pieces together as to what triggers my depression. I've decided that I make the mistake of keeping stressful and emotional events to myself. I tend to let one event build upon another and feel overwhelmed, not wanting to share or admit my irrational thoughts with anyone, allowing depression to take over.

Having read a lot about MS, attended seminars, listened to doctors and research scientists, etc., I have learned that despite the challenges MS may bring, there are ways to manage many of the bizarre symptoms I (and others) experience.

Neurologists and your family doctor, for example, are able to make specific suggestions for treatment and can also make referrals to various professionals who specialize in other areas of care—for example, a urologist, physical therapist, occupational therapist, eye specialist, psychologist, etc.

It's important to know there are tools to enhance memory. There are ways to minimize the effects of heat and ways to manage bladder and bowel issues, balance, pain, sensory symptoms, fatigue, depression, and more.

Even though I didn't want to talk to a counselor, I thank God that Bob and my daughters insisted. Dawn actually picked me up out of bed and put me in my chair. I really felt sorry for the counselor because I spoke about five words during my first appointment. I guess you could say I wasn't willing to open up at that point.

My prayers and my family's were answered as each month I willingly shared my irrational thoughts and concerns with my counselor Barb. I'm very thankful for my understanding family and friends, for the knowledge and wisdom of professionals, and especially for God's presence in my life—for his gentle nudge.

Like the experience of many other patients, throughout the course of my disease, my neurologist has prescribed specific medications to temporarily treat specific symptoms. Because there's no cure, doctors' hands are tied (so to speak); thus they do their best to treat specific issues.

It was about twenty years ago that my doctor suggested the intravenous treatment of cytoxine (a common cancer procedure). It was documented to benefit some MS patients. He told me that of all his patients who had finished this treatment, 50 percent reported signs of improvement. Even though I knew I would lose my hair, I agreed to give it a try. I believe in the phrase no pain, no gain.

When I went for my two-week follow-up appointment (wearing a wig), I simply said I was sorry that I didn't fall into his 50 percent of improvement. By the look on his face, I could tell he was very disappointed on my behalf.

The most unconventional treatment (not suggested by my neurologist) was stings from honeybees. You must be wondering why on earth would I agree to such an unconventional therapy. Well, after I watched a *Dateline* program featuring a lady (with MS) applying honeybees to MSers' arms, legs, spinal cord, etc., my interest was sparked. Realizing that this treatment does not come with a 100 percent guarantee of decreasing everyone's symptoms, it was encouraging to learn that it had positive results with some patients. At this point I'll share the reaction of my neurologist (Springfield, MA Doctor M). Knowing his personality, I was not the least bit offended when he laughed at my choice. I was actually following his guide rules and doing something I knew was not harmful—just very unusual, according to the AMA.

It was my good friend George Wallace (a respected retired principal of our local high school) who was eager to persuade me to give it a try. George was an active, and avid, beekeeper for many years. He had read many articles on the bee venom therapy for MS patients and gave me the papers to read for myself.

Before I agreed to commit myself to this treatment, I realized there were several good reasons why it made sense to give it a try, such as: I didn't have to go out of the country to do it, I didn't have to pay anything for the bees, and finally, no one was promising me positive results. Before George placed the first bee on my forearm, he led us in prayer. I knew that deep in his heart, he hoped that I would once again be able to walk.

The process of bee stings is really fascinating—painful yes, but fascinating. Using a pair of tongs, my husband would put one bee at a time onto my skin. Immediately he would remove the bee, but the stinger remained, pumping its venom into my skin. Each day I would increase the number of stings—one a day, three a day, five a day, and up to twenty at a time. At the end of my treatment (winter), I had taken a total of three hundred stings.

My end-of-treatment results were not quite what George had hoped for, but I did reassure him I did experience more stamina and strength. Unfortunately, these encouraging results didn't remain for long. However, I do not regret trying this unusual treatment.

It was in 1980 that I hired our very first cleaning lady. Having been diagnosed with a herniated disc, I found that vacuuming and other household tasks were becoming too difficult. My choice was not to overburden my husband and daughters with additional responsibilities. So common sense prompted me to hire a cleaning lady.

Through the years, I've been fortunate to find capable, honest, and reliable ladies. Unfortunately, this is not the result that always occurs. If this is a service you require, I have found that referrals from friends and family members are most often successful. However, I have learned the hard way and regret to say that I once discovered a woman had been stealing prescription meds, and another had been stealing money from me. Needless to say, I terminated their work for me.

I have been told that some people providing care for others do not like to be referred to as caregivers. Regarding this, I've known people who are PCAs (personal care attendants). Most often, I refer to my ladies as my helpers (and as a friend). Now that I'm no longer driving my van, these women have also become my chauffeurs (something like *Driving Miss Daisy*).

With all the possible symptoms associated with multiple sclerosis, I actually believe this disease has made me a better person. Life's challenges have taught me to not take my blessings for granted, nor the people whom God has placed in my life.

Quite often I have said I do some things in an odd way, but the end result is still accomplished. In order for me to succeed, a lot of times, I've had to think outside the box. For example, I know that it's against the law to drink and drive; however, I've been known to drive my scooter while gripping onto a paper cup with my teeth. Yes, it may look strange, but it works for me.

I would like to end this chapter by passing on a suggestion given to me by Rev. John Post. Having heard me ask a friend for a cup of coffee (in Fellowship Hall after worship), he suggested I make my request differently. John thought I should say, "May I afford you the opportunity of pouring me a cup of coffee?" I have used this suggestion many times since 1978 when John first suggested it to me.

CHAPTER 7

Life in a Wheelchair

I've never lost the ownership paper for my car while street racing, nor have I lost any money during Texas-holdem tournaments, and I've never made any bets on sporting-game predictions. However, if I were to take a poll of fifty people and ask how many would willingly sit in a wheelchair twenty-four seven, I'll bet you any amount of money that not one person would agree to do this—unless it was absolutely necessary, that is.

One of the reasons I agreed to use a manual wheelchair was because of a common-sense issue. In 1980 we planned a vacation cruise. When getting ready to go, my biggest quandary was: Do I take the chance of falling down (hurting myself and needing someone to pick me up) OR do I use a wheelchair and therefore enable myself to have a great time without stitches or loss of blood?

The many people I've met who have been diagnosed with multiple sclerosis and are ambulatory make every effort (by the use of a leg brace, an exercise routine, medications, etc.) to avoid the use of a wheelchair. Can you blame them?

I would say there are several reasons for this way of thinking. It could be their feelings of loss (not being able to walk). It can also be a matter of pride (not wanting anyone to see them relying upon a wheel chair)—maybe feeling less of a man, for instance, and wanting to be the breadwinner, etc. Maybe they don't want people to stare at them. My answer to this last reason, when it happens to me, is that I just assume they are admiring my hair. Sounds good to me.

Another reason for wanting to avoid the use of a wheelchair could be that people sometimes make a very serious (incorrect) assumption. On this, I can speak from experience. Some people assume that you are not only physically disabled but that you must be mentally disabled as well. This is very evident when adults speak down to you thinking that you are incapable of understanding. It's not a good feeling.

One of my favorite stories to tell is of me (with my sister-in-law standing behind me) sitting up against the airline check-in counter. As I looked up at the clerk (we were so close I could have touched her), she proceeded to ask my sister-in-law if she (I) would like to sit in first class. My issue with this is that she could have very easily asked me, the passenger. I was so tempted to say to her, "Why on earth would I want to fly first class? By all means, give the seat to someone else." After I said that I'd appreciate changing my seat, I enjoyed the free wine, the real china and utensils, and especially the wide and comfy seat.

When I stop to think about it, there was another very good reason as to why no one had to twist my arm, or force me, to use a wheelchair. I had taken quite a few falls resulting in deep cuts on my head.

I clearly remember staying up late one night to watch the local news. My husband, Paul, had already gone to bed. On the way to the bedroom, I leaned against the walls in order to keep my balance. Not wanting to wake him up, I left the light off and balanced myself along the dresser. I was doing just fine until my hand slipped off the edge. Needless to say, I fell down, and my head hit the edge of the bathroom door. Not wanting to cause alarm, I convinced myself that the cut didn't warrant a 911 phone call. In the morning there was blood on my pillow and my pajama sleeve, and some had dripped off the door onto the floor.

After the fact, I thought, my hair was going to thin out sooner or later. I didn't need more scar tissue to speed up the process of a bald head. Soooo, my willingness to utilize the wheelchair just seemed like good common sense. I didn't necessarily have to like it, I simply needed to adjust to it and make the best of it.

For many people, the wheelchair comes with the stigma of doom and gloom. I seriously believe that this needn't be the case in every situation. To contradict that thought, I have willingly taken an active part in many situations that, once again, support my declaration for possibilities of life after MS. Going far back into the history of America, I'm reminded of President Franklin D. Roosevelt and his service to Americans—seated in a wheelchair.

While sitting in my electric scooter, I am thankful to say that I have been able to attend my granddaughters' dance recitals and field days; sing in the church choir (they built a ramp); attend concerts; take flights to Minnesota, Seattle, California, Florida, Jamaica, London etc.; circle my house as my four-year-old grand twins chased me; and act in my church's Murder Mystery Dinner Theater for ten years.

My first character in the play was a motorcycle babe from the Blandford Burger and Brew. For sure, I made people laugh, and I have so many fond memories of the fun we had playing a variety of characters. Did I mention I once portrayed an exercise director on a cruise ship—sweat band, spandex, and all? Then I'm wondering how many women have ever addressed their pastor as "sweet cheeks." Before you judge me too harshly, I must say that I simply said what was in the script. Actually, I did change the wording just a tad. If I'm not mistaken, this comes under the category of artistic license. I have no doubt that when addressing clergy, the only member who would say sweet cheeks would be the spouse. As much as I could go on and on with my escapades, I will cease.

I've already described my trip to Minnesota in order to attend a high school reunion. When I received the invitation, including instructions to write about my life after graduation, I gave careful thought as to what I would say. My concern was that because of my wheelchair, I didn't want to travel that distance to simply sit in a corner and be ignored. As I mentioned, people may want to talk to you but choose not to because they're afraid of saying the wrong thing. I seriously wanted them to know that I was still the same person. I just couldn't play volleyball anymore.

I am pleased to say that for years, my scooter has enabled me to visit a nearby hospital that houses a neurological wing. The majority of patients living there have multiple sclerosis and can no longer be cared for at home.

Going to the hospital for my first visit, I sat in each person's doorway and asked, "Would you like a visitor?" Nobody refused. As I approached each person, I introduced myself and explained that I had also been diagnosed with MS. Needless to say, our conversations flowed easily as they explained their backgrounds. We had much in common, and they looked forward to my next visit as much as I did.

These people have become my friends, and I've always felt blessed to share with them. One lady in particular, Barb, really touched my heart. After her very long battle with MS, bedridden and unable to speak, she smiled and brightened up the room each time I sat with her. What an inspiration she was for me and others.

"God's Wheelchair" is the title of an article taken from the May 30, 2012 issue of *Our Daily Bread*. The theme was taken from Daniel 7:9: "His throne was a fiery flame, its wheels a burning fire."

Jean Driscoll is the person of interest in this brief article. Described as a remarkable athlete, she has won the Boston Marathon and has taken part in four Paralympics Games. Jean was born with spina bifida and competes in her wheelchair.

Daniel 7:9, is Jean's favorite Bible passage. She sees a connection between Daniel's vision of God and her own situation. It is because of this passage that she is able to pass along words of encouragement to others. She has said that when talking to people in wheelchairs, if they feel bad about being in a chair, she tells them: "Not only are you made in the image of God, but your wheelchair is made in the image of his throne!" Faith in God has helped Jean triumph over personal challenges. We can be confident that the high and holy one is near and ready to help us if only we ask.

I would like to share with you a short poem found within this same article. It reads:

He cannot fail, your faithful God;

He'll guard you with His mighty power;

Then fear no ill though troubles rise,

His help is sure from hour to hour. —Bosch

As I have often driven my car over speed bumps on roadways, my thoughts are that life itself is full of speed bumps in one form or another: challenges, roadblocks, adjustments to change and loss, etc. The choices we make regarding these unexpected glitches will impact our lives greatly and of those we love dearly.

I constantly remind myself that life is shaped by the daily choices I make. Do I wake up and decide to be bitter and angry about my situation, or do I come to my senses and make the best of what I have? When I stop and think of all the people who have health issues far more severe than mine (Barb), I thank God for what I CAN DO and count my blessings.

CHAPTER 8

Wheelchair Travel Adventures

Hold on to your hats as I share some dandy travel stories I've experienced and explain how I've learned (the hard way) to ask the right questions before I pack my suitcase.

As I think way back to my pre-MS traveling days, I remind myself that then, I never had to think about: Will the airline allow my electric wheelchair on board, will the airline staff help me into my seat, will I be allowed to pack a supply of daily injections (copaxone), is the hotel wheelchair accessible, does the bed have a clearance of seven inches underneath for Bob's Hoyer-lift, do they have an accessible bathroom, does it have a roll-in shower stall, will I be able to rent a handicap van with a ramp, will I need to rent a portable ramp from a nearby medical supply store in order to enter homes with stairs etc., etc.?

As my symptoms have slowly progressed, these details came into play. Having been a secretary, I actually enjoy the planning and scheduling. However, it was just lately that I discovered AAA doesn't just repair flat tires and jump start car batteries. Making use of my membership status, I can have AAA reserve a handicap van, arrange for a portable ramp, and even make hotel reservations.

My husband's business trip to London (1990) allowed me to go as well at no additional cost. We simply exchanged his first-class ticket for two seats in the coach section. Touring several historical sites, watching the queen's birthday parade (with Princess Diana and Charles), drinking beer in a neighborhood pub, etc., was very enjoyable. Touring St. Paul's Cathedral was a delight; we looked forward to it. As we got off the tour bus, our guide simply asked that we return in two hours. Even before we saw the inside of the cathedral, our trip to the front door was beyond unbelievable. Uff-da, for sure.

After we saw the long stairway, our first thought was to look for an elevator. Having failed to find any hint of easy access, my husband proceeded to lift me (backward) up every single step. I think it was then that my fond memories of Lady Di's flowing bridal gown flowing up this stairway were deleted from my memory bank. Having no broken bones or open wounds, we rested a bit before entering the lovely cathedral.

You're not going to believe what one of the priests said to us before we entered the door. He simply said, "Be sure to let me know when you are leaving, and I will show you to our elevator." I seriously believe that it was then that the drool gushed out of our dropped jaws. I'm afraid we hesitated before giving our guide a tip (other than suggesting she be better prepared).

I remember doing something (in my chair) that was probably not allowed (borderline illegal) while rushing from one airplane gate to another.

Before I explain myself, I'd like you to know I'm fully aware of the proper use of an escalator. However, to save us more time, my husband placed my front wheels on the escalator while standing behind me holding my chair up until we safely got off. The intelligent observer would more than likely say that I had failed to set a good example for young children. What can I say? My thoughts are that you do what you have to do sometimes.

Is your motel wheelchair assessable? In order to attend an evangelism seminar, this was the question I asked before making reservations. Unfortunately, after the fact, I had to remind myself to never assume anything.

Having arrived at the motel and going into my room, I quickly realized what their definition of wheelchair assessable meant. Yes, I could enter through the front door, and I could enter my room. But as I attempted to get my chair through the bathroom door, I found that it was not wide enough. Thankfully I could stand, hold onto the counter, and inch my way to the toilet. I warn you not to make the same mistake I did. You must be very thorough and specific with your questions before making reservations.

While visiting the Mall of America, I rented an electric wheelchair to avoid the need for Jan (my cousin) to push my manual chair around for ten miles (I do exaggerate). I quickly discovered a metal box attached to the handle of the rental chair. For me to go into reverse, I had to press a button and hold it until I stopped.

Normally, I do my best to not be conspicuous. I have a very good feeling that you know exactly why this button needed to be pressed. You're right—a very LOUD beeping sound was heard every time I had to back up. Needless to say, I purposely avoided driving in reverse unless it was absolutely necessary to do so.

When exiting the bathroom stall at Nordstrom's department store (tiled floors, tiled walls, tiled ceilings), I sounded like an eighteen-wheeler. The beeping sound must have echoed throughout the store. As one of my T-shirts states, "I laughed so hard that tears ran down my leg." That was a day that Jan and I will long remember. We can tell this to our friends at "the home" years from now. Ho ho.

While on vacation, is it really out of the question to roll your wheelchair through the sandy beaches and into the water? More often than not, the answer would be that this is impossible. "Au contraire," I say.

If you take time to ask a travel agent, AAA office, or lifeguard office, etc., you may very well locate a beach that offers balloon-tire wheelchairs. My first experience with this type of chair was at Hampden Beach, Massachusetts. What an awesome experience it was for me, putting my feet in the ocean, thanks to this special chair and my son-in-law Rob.

I've been known to say the only reason people want to travel with me seems fairly obvious: they don't have to wait in long lines (Disneyland and Sea World, for example), and they also get very good parking spots. Well yes, I do suspect there are some nicer reasons as well.

At first, when I didn't know why wheelchair occupants didn't have to wait in lines, I couldn't help but notice other tourists staring at me. I actually felt a bit guilty. These feelings vanished as I became aware that safety issues were the determining factor. I could easily visualize myself sitting in the middle of a crowd when an emergency evacuation was ordered. Truth be, people would trip over me and possibly be trampled in the chaos, causing serious injury to me and others.

I feel compelled to say that yes, sometimes I do take liberties (take advantage of) being in a wheelchair. I tend to say that people usually feel sorry for old ladies sitting in a wheelchair (67). A few examples: being offered first-class seating when an opening is available; getting good seating at theaters-museums; and getting re-assigned seating in the coach section of an airplane, allowing me more space to get on and off the plane.

Locating the bathrooms is one of the very first things you may want to do at restaurants, etc. Even when I wasn't pregnant, a full bladder (not being able to control it) was a frequent issue. In my case, if the ladies' bathroom was not assessable (downstairs, upstairs, etc.) my husband would secure the men's room door, and then he was able to help me.

To tell you the truth, the men's room situation has happened to me so many times that I really couldn't give you an accurate count. This was quite often the case when we visited London. I do hope that I didn't give American women a tarnished reputation. Of course you know that I am only joking (the reputation part). Today, I am happy to say that most airports, amusement parks etc., have a family bathroom. These facilities are wheelchair assessable and are open to men and women.

Despite the fact twenty years have gone by, I vividly remember a flight to San Diego. The experience I'm going to share with you deals with the airplane's bathroom and my getting into it.

Before I begin, I want to repeat that I don't really mind when people stare at me. The fact is that I was unable to walk well, and I needed my husband's help getting to the bathroom. So he stood in the aisle, and I wrapped my arms around his neck. As I held on for dear life, he carried me while walking backward to the nearest bathroom.

This airline bathroom saga continues. Would you ever think that a 200-pound man and a 120-pound woman can lock the door behind them in an airline bathroom? It's even hard for me to believe that we actually did that without the door bursting open. How embarrassing would that be? I'd surely meet a lot of new people.

Speaking of airline flights, I will venture to say that nobody has ever done what I once did. "What would that be?" you say. To sit in my assigned seat, I went down the aisle sitting on a very narrow aisle chair (very narrow). While I was being pulled backward, I suddenly wondered why my left leg was wet. Because the aisles are so very narrow, the lock on my catheter bag was accidentally forced open as my leg bumped against a seat. It was at that moment I saw the perfectly straight line (of urine) before my eyes. If I had been wearing slacks, the wetness would have been obvious to everyone. Fortunately I was wearing capris and only needed to clean my lower leg. Uff-da!

To help alleviate some of my guilt, I felt confident this stain would be cleaned along with spilled coffee, puddles of baby food, etc., etc.

When traveling, there have been times that I had no choice—I had to use a glass-walled elevator. Most often when this occurs, it seems rather obvious that people quickly move their feet back. I do my best to reassure them that I am a good driver. The last thing I say to them, however, is that they don't have to be afraid because I only run over people I know (family, etc.). This works every time. The people can relax and usually laugh.

I have been known to say that if I had been single for the last forty-five years of my life, meeting men would never have been a problem for me. It's because of my traveling, for one reason or another, that men have come to my assistance even without my having to ask.

Men have picked me up and carried me to be seated in roller coaster seats, passenger seats in cars and airplanes, horse carriages, a small private airplane, couches, exercise table, hayride wagons, camping trailer, tour buses, etc. etc.

Having taken part in my church's mission trips to South Carolina, my friend Kevin offered to help seat me in my van. I have known Kevin and his wife Judy for many years. Knowing his sense of humor, I couldn't resist asking him, "And just where do you think you're going to put those hands?" Yes he laughed and then simply ignored the concerned look on my face. Obviously, I didn't intimidate him in the least.

Smear toothpaste on my fanny? Please let me explain the circumstances of this bizarre question. It was when a friend of mine (Carol) and I went to Cape Cod to visit a mutual friend (Caroline) that each of them took turns getting me ready for bed. One night I made the request of putting a special cream on my bottom. Just as the tube had been grabbed and applied, I couldn't help wondering why my skin was burning (must have been the fluoride). When we realized that the toothpaste tube had been used, I couldn't stop myself from laughing hysterically. My friend was very apologetic, needless to say, but I reassured her I was fine (after washing) and that this had been one the funniest things that had ever happened to me—and continued to laugh.

Never assume anything is a suggestion I have already made (when will I ever learn?). This thought comes to mind as I remember taking a very short trip to visit a friend (female). Just as I was about to leave my in-laws' apartment, my lap was covered with bags, and I knew my caregivers had a few more things to carry to the car as well.

Having arrived at my friend's home, I made a horrific discovery. My suitcase was still in my apartment. Thankfully I didn't need fancy clothing, so I easily took care of this dilemma. We went to Kmart and purchased shorts, tops, undies, etc. For pajamas, my friend gave me a pair of hers, and four years later they are still in my drawer. When I wear them, I'm fondly reminded of this trip.

If at all possible, I would highly suggest traveling. Depending on the amount of time you have, your getaways could be one- or two-day trips, a long weekend, or a complete week. These excursions get you out of the house (a change of scenery) and offer a healthy and relaxing change to your daily routine.

As I have shared just a few traveling experiences of my own, I'm sure you will agree that quite often some specific preparation is needed to ensure a more enjoyable time away. While away, there have been many times I have said, "The only decision I want to make on vacation is: Do I want a hamburger or cheeseburger?" I'm away from my home phone and have no meetings to attend. Ah, such peace.

CHAPTER 9

Let Me Tell You about Bob

Having been married to my first husband, Paul, for thirty-six years, without any warning I became a widow on November 3, 2002. It was when Paul was in the midst of using his rowing machine that he suffered a fatal heart attack.

Needless to say, very abruptly my emotions ran rampant while I faced drastic changes and loss in my life. Without my daughters, friends, and extended family, I could have very easily slipped into a severe depression. I did, however, experience a mild depression (diagnosed by a counselor). He prescribed a mild antidepressant, and it helped me immensely with the depression issue.

I'm being very honest when I say that getting remarried had never entered my mind. While keeping myself busy (in my in-laws' apartment) there did come a time when I actually thought, Why would any man want to marry an older lady confined to a wheelchair? This thought came to mind not because I had low self-esteem, but because it seemed like a very realistic thought. However, I reminded myself that it is God who's in charge of my marital status, not me alone.

It was in December 2007 that I wondered if my longtime friend (Bob Berwaldt) was still alive. Really, I didn't know for sure. I did know that his MS symptoms had progressed more seriously than mine, so it made me wonder how he was doing.

Throughout the past, I had called Bob every once in a while just to see how he was or to discuss MS business. Close to the upcoming Christmas holiday, for instance, I'd call to remind him to send in his reservation for the dinner party. I always enjoyed our conversations and my ability to make him laugh. Before I tell you in detail about our phone conversation, I'd like to explain how and why we became acquainted in the first place.

It was in December 1976 that my family and I moved to Massachusetts, from Pennsylvania. Having gotten boxes and suitcases unpacked, beds put together, and our daughter enrolled in school, etc., my goal was to speak to the office manager of the Springfield National MS Society when time allowed me to do so.

Sr. Mary Dennis (also diagnosed with MS) answered the telephone, and I explained who I was, that I had recently moved to Massachusetts, and that I wanted to know if there was an existing monthly MS support group and if so, how would I get there. She told me there was no such group at the time, but thought had been given to establishing a support group in the future.

Upon her suggestion, I continued to call Sr. Mary Dennis with this same question from time to time. I was so very happy when I received her call telling me that a nearby nursing home would allow us to use one of their rooms for meetings. I was able to drive, so I picked up a few ladies, and Sr. Mary Dennis had invited men and women (including spouses and caregivers).

Our support group met for at least seven months, sharing personal experiences and concerns and asking questions. It's not very often that your best friend or next-door neighbor is living with MS and can share issues or exacerbations or fully understand what you are going through.

I'll never forget the day I received the horrific phone call from Sr. Mary Dennis. Nearly in tears, she said that she had just gotten a phone call and was ordered to shut down the office and to lock the door. We were both outraged with this news and agreed that we should try to do something about it. My immediate thought was, when people in our group need help, do they wheel themselves (on the highway) to the Hartford, Connecticut, office? I don't think so!

St. Mary Dennis scheduled a task force to brainstorm ideas on how to legally incorporate our own independent monthly support group. Our group was composed of Sr. Dennis, me, and four more MSers. During our conversation, a man named Robert Berwaldt told us he knew of a lawyer who might be willing to help us with the legalities of this process. And yes, this was the day that Bob and I first met.

Much to our surprise, our group was overjoyed to learn that incorporating such a group was now easily within our grasp. Not only did this lawyer (David) help us with the legalities, he volunteered his services to us free of charge. God is good!

David told us that to incorporate a support group, it was necessary for us to elect officers (president, vice president, treasurer, and secretary) and put together a board of trustees. After a vote, Bob became president, and I became secretary.

Our board was composed of a pastor, a neurologist, and a lawyer, and it met once a month. Bob was in charge of our support group for the first ten years, and then I facilitated the group for the next ten years while Bob began work on behalf of handicap advocacy affairs.

I'm proud to say that the support group is still active and led by other capable people. These groups are vital for sharing and comparing personal thoughts and concerns, side effects of medication, etc. This support group has served hundreds of people over the years.

Those in attendance were people newly diagnosed, those diagnosed years ago, family members, caregivers, and friends. Our meetings were open to anyone wanting to learn and share their experiences and concerns of MS.

Every now and then, a local college instructor would call me to ask whether or not one of their nursing or psychology students could sit in at one of our meetings. We welcomed the students knowing that they would gain firsthand information (right from the trenches, so to speak).

Now I will tell you more about my phone call to Bob on that fateful December day of 2007 and of how our relationship developed into more than a mere friendship.

If you're expecting a steamy love story (Fabio on the cover, etc.), that's not what you're about to read in this book. I've jokingly said to Bob that when we first met, I didn't exactly want to pounce on him even though he was a good-looking man. With all due respect, we were both married to other people at the time. To pounce on him then would have been highly frowned upon, don't you agree? Uff-da! What would people think? And then, I have serious thoughts that our spouses would really not have approved. Mmmmm?

Following the usual pleasantries (how are you, what have you been up to, how's your family? etc.), I learned that Bob was divorced, and Bob learned that I had become a widow.

After learning these new bits of information about each other, we continued talking—and talking, and talking. At the end of our conversation, I had gotten an invitation to have dinner at Bob's house. I tell people that was when Bob began to chase me (until I caught him). You're absolutely right; I have no shame.

Our friendship began in the late seventies, both working for a common cause: to establish a monthly support group in the Springfield area. As fellow officers, we worked on a monthly newsletter, planning Christmas parties and summer picnics, selecting guest speakers, etc. Bob and I didn't know it at the time, but our wise and loving God knew that we would be married on November 8, 2008. I have no doubt of this whatsoever.

One of the reasons our phone call lasted so long (2007) is that because of our history, we had a great deal in common. Over the years we had both met countless numbers of people. In attendance each month there were spouses and caregivers with newly diagnosed MS patients eager to learn and share common experiences.

Over the years, Bob and I (and others) learned how much we were alike and also how much our MS experience differed from the rest. We all understood why some members used canes, crutches, walkers, and wheelchairs. We shared a common bond. We knew that this complicated, mysterious, and most often cruel disease was the common denominator that we shared.

Bob and I agree that there was definitely a great need for a local support group. Newly diagnosed people, and their care-givers, benefit greatly when they can ask other people questions such as who's your neurologist, how long have you been diagnosed, what medications have you taken, did you lose your job because of the MS, is your family supportive, etc.?

When Bob and I first met, I was impressed by his leadership skills, his knowledge, and his healthy sense of humor. These were important qualities needed to facilitate our newly formed support group (Pioneer Valley MS Association).

It was not very long after our monthly meetings were established that Bob became good friends with Phil (also one of the people who helped to incorporate our group). How does the saying go that perfectly describes this pair? Oh yes—it's the quiet ones you have to be careful of. For sure, that fits them to a *T*. Let me give you just one example that supports my determination of these two.

While I was doing something in my kitchen one day, the telephone rang. I emptied my hands and answered the phone. It took me only a few seconds to realize that I was talking to an encyclopedia salesman. Rather than quickly saying no thank you and goodbye, I was patient and listened to his scripted spiel for a few minutes.

As the sales pitch seemed to go on and on, I simply apologized and told him that I had to hang up. Before I could even finish my sentence, this man blurted out, "Ma'am, how dare you be so rude." Not believing my ears, I said, "I beg your pardon" as I slammed the phone on the wall. I was so angry that I thought I was going to rip the phone off the wall. I was so flustered that I kept on saying "I don't believe it" for hours.

It was two hours after that horrific phone call that my phone began to ring again. As soon as I picked it up, a man's voice said, "Hi, Vickie, this is Phil. Could I interest you in a set of encyclopedias?" After I told him that he was horrible and rotten, I began to laugh—and laugh, and laugh.

The very same night, I was scheduled to meet with other officers at Phil's house. Because of my earlier phone call, I felt compelled to get even with him. Before I left home, I called Phil's wife to explain what I was going to do at their house (to retaliate). Before the meeting was called to order, I asked Phil to show me where his phone was. Rather than pick up the receiver, I took a hacksaw and pretended to cut the cord in half. "Now, you won't be able to call me—not ever."

Just recently, Bob and I saw Phil at a veterans' social event. Before I even said hello to him, I reminded him of what a horrible person I thought he was. Needless to say, thirty years later (the encyclopedia sales attempt), we both still laugh about it. Until this very day, Bob denies being a part of that telephone prank. It must be that because I know Bob is very capable of such a gag, I seriously think that he was actually in on it.

Because our group met once a month (summers off) for twenty years, several friendships were formed. When introducing themselves at meetings and saying where they lived, some people found that the person sitting next to them was a nearby neighbor. The situation happened more than once, to our surprise.

More than once I have told you that Bob has a very healthy sense of humor. I will never (never) forget, prior to our wedding, when Bob and I were sitting on the sofa on a Sunday afternoon. As I attempted to kiss him, he very convincingly and seriously told me that his church did not approve of members kissing on Sundays. Because of the fact that I really didn't know everything about the Baptist Church, I very hesitantly believed him. So there I sat, minding my Ps and Qs, not approaching him for an hour.

Would you believe that he actually wondered why I was so standoffish. It was then that I reminded him of his church not condoning kissing on Sundays. After he stopped laughing (and laughing), I told him what a creep he was. I then told this story to members of Bob's church, and they did the very same thing. They laughed. It's nearly four years after the fact, and I continue to remind him of his cruel prank. My motive for doing this is probably just that I like to see him laugh.

I have often told Bob that he reminds me a lot of my deceased brother. Other than both being really good guys, I am specifically speaking of their facial expressions. Just as I could with my brother, I can look at Bob's wrinkled brow and sheepish grin and know something very odd is going to come out of his mouth. It's almost as though you can see smoke coming out of his ears. Without a doubt, I know he's about to say or do something very strange.

I've told you about my awesome daughters Lynn and Dawn, their husbands (sons-in-law Trevor and Rob), AND grandchildren: Jasmine (12) and Keera Ann and Brady (5). And yes, I now am blessed with stepdaughters Karen and Jessica (awesome as well), giving me two more sons-in-law (John and Jeff). For an added bonus, I have Brian, Andy, Jack, and Jake as my terrific step-grandsons.

Before I focus on the next chapter, I want to share one thought regarding our engagement. Once again sitting on Bob's sofa, he asked me to marry him. The first words that came out of my mouth were, "What took you so long?" Obviously (and thankfully), he correctly translated that to mean YES!

CHAPTER 10

Wheelchair Wedding

Where do I begin? is the first question I asked when planning my first wedding in 1966. If it were not for my mom and mother-in-law-to-be, as well as sisters-in-law and girlfriends, that wedding may have taken place at the justice of the peace chapel. Instead, this ceremony took place in my church (Lutheran Church of the Good Shepherd), followed by cake and coffee in fellowship hall. My mother and I couldn't afford an expensive or elaborate wedding.

As each of my daughters planned her wedding, I did whatever I could to help them when asked to do so. I did my very best, however, to never say, "You shouldn't do it that way, you should do it this way." I put myself in their place, knowing that I would dread hearing those words myself.

So with all of these wedding planning experiences under my belt, I felt confident when preparing a to-do list for my wedding to Bob. To tell you the truth, I had the feeling that Bob would have liked the wedding to happen sooner rather than later. Yes, I guess you could say that he was anxious. However, I explained my desire to plan for more than just cake and coffee at our reception.

Because of the time restraints and my ability to work on five things a time, I made quick decisions on several matters. I kept Bob up to date at all times, knowing that I could make changes if need be.

Bob's favorite part of the planning was the wedding cake sampling session. We decided on a three-layer cake, each layer a different flavor. Each of us chose a favorite flavor and agreed on the third layer. The final cake was not only beautiful, it was delicious as well.

I have no doubt that most of you, women especially, know the routine of preparing for a wedding. Our to-do list consisted of: confirm the pastors (Bob's and mine); reserve the church; reserve a reception room; select flowers, cake, and table decorations; and decide on our bridal party. Our daughters Lynn, Dawn, Karen, and Jessica were my bridesmaids. Bob chose his groomsmen (husbands of the bridesmaids), and we asked three of his grandsons to usher. The fourth was our ring bearer. Our flower girl was my eight-year-old granddaughter Jasmine.

Continuing the task of confirming bridal party members, I proceeded to call my cousin Jan (Iowa). After talking for just a few minutes, I asked her if she could check her calendar for November 8. After she told me that she had no special plans, I said to her, "What would you think of being my maid of honor once again?" Not even knowing of our wedding plans, she quickly said, "Of course!"

I then made a similar call to my brother, Milan. When he confirmed that his calendar was open for November 8, I said, "What would you think of walking me down the aisle again?" Like Jan, he said, "Of course!" The only vacant spot was Bob's best man, and he chose his cousin Cliff (New York). Our all-family bridal party was awesome and provided very fond memories for everyone.

The process of thinking outside the box now came into play once again. At my first wedding, just like nearly every other bride, I carried a lovely bouquet down the aisle. For this wedding, however, I would need both of my hands to steer my scooter. Running into pews and guests would have been highly frowned upon, and because of their injuries, they'd be unable to dance at the reception. Uff-da!

Sooo, I asked a very talented friend from church (Betty) to craft a circular arrangement of silk flowers that we attached to the front of my scooter. Indeed this was not the norm, but it did the trick and the bouquet was lovely. Betty also made a small bouquet that I would later throw to the eager unmarried women.

Oh yes, what about my wedding dress? Regarding this topic, whenever Bob hears me talking about eBay, he simply looks at me and laughs. Yes, I will tell you why he thinks my story is so funny. Really, he basically enjoys teasing me.

Knowing that I didn't want to buy an expensive white gown (or any expensive dress), once again I turned on my trusty computer. Not really knowing much about eBay, I got into this Web site having been told that a person can get really good deals. I chose the category of women's gowns and proceeded to look for an appropriate dress in autumn colors.

My search was a success, I found the perfect dress. Not only did I like the dress, I really liked the low price, which was fifty dollars. Another incentive was the fact that the dress was new and was worth two hundred dollars. Knowing that I had to bid against other prospective buyers, I increased my bid to sixty dollars. Because I really wanted the dress, I kept raising my bid periodically. With my final offer of one hundred dollars, I bought the dress.

I will now share (reluctantly) one of my most embarrassing moments. Having told Bob that I was bidding for a dress on eBay and that I was increasing the amount over three or four days, he said to me (with a grin on his face), "Vickie, you've been bidding against yourself." I said, "Really?" I was really embarrassed knowing that I could have saved myself fifty dollars. What a lesson that was for me. Once again, I say Uff-da.

There was now yet another necessity that would require an uncustomary choice. Yes, the cake topper. After looking in party-equipment stores, grocery stores, and bakeries, I discovered that there were not any toppers with either the bride or groom (or both) in a wheelchair. With my limited computer skills, I began to search the Internet for toppers with wheelchairs. Being persistent, I found one with the groom sitting in the chair and the bride sitting on his lap. Perfect!

When the UPS driver delivered the topper to my door, my arts and crafts skills kicked into overdrive. Using my craft paints, I made the bride's dress and bouquet match mine and the groom's suit and tie match Bob's. These small details made me very happy.

While working on the cake topper, I began to think about our reception. In particular, I thought about the opening dance of the bride and groom. It really didn't take me much time at all to solve this issue. I simply asked one of Bob's helpers (strong and with a healthy back) if he would pick me up and set me on Bob's lap (just like the cake topper). Leave it to me to suggest that it might be a good idea to practice this several times before the wedding. Hmmmm.

Continuing the subject of the bride and groom's dance, I never gave thought to the fact that I would be wearing a dress made of a very slippery fabric. I'm pretty sure you know exactly where this story's going. Yes, as Bob drove his chair in circles, Dawn was busy pushing me up onto his lap each time I began to slide down. And to think I hadn't even had my usual four margaritas (yet).

Having agreed that the ceremony would take place at my church, I thought about the fact that there was one step up to the altar. Actually, even though Bob and I were both in wheelchairs, this one step did not cause a stressful problem. You see, I'd been a member of the choir for many years and had been able to do so because of a custom-made ramp.

My only concern at this point was to make sure Bob could safely drive his chair up this ramp without falling off the edge. Good grief!

Not really wanting to think about Bob falling, I think you'd agree that his crashing on the floor would certainly have made our wedding memorable (for all the wrong reasons). To make matters worse, while waiting for the emergency room doctor to sign Bob's release papers, we would have been really late for the reception. That calls for a big Uff-da!

I say that's enough thinking about the emergency room (blood, stitches, bandages, etc.). Our focus was now on partying, food, dancing, and fun. To the benefit of everyone in attendance, we accomplished our goal with an emphasis on fun, with flying colors. I was later told that I didn't drive too fast when leading the conga line.

Despite the few customized formalities of our wedding ceremony and reception (just going with the flow), I'm very happy to say that Bob and I are legally married and will soon celebrate our fourth anniversary—this calls for more food, celebration, and fun. As is often said in Minnesota, you betcha!

CHAPTER 11

Summary

More than anything else, my desire for this book has been to give some peace of mind to newly diagnosed MS people, their families, and friends. From my own experience, I'd like to ease your fears of the unknown and any unnecessary stress as best I can. The anguish my mother experienced is an emotion I'd like you to avoid. I seriously believe "there is life after MS!" I genuinely hope you will agree that this positive thought is well worth striving for. It is most certainly worth your time and effort.

Just as there are specific stages of grief (anger, denial, grieving, etc.) a person may experience after a death, a newly diagnosed person often goes through the very same grieving process.

Anguish and uncertainty are primarily caused by the well-known fact that multiple sclerosis is an extremely complicated and incurable neurological disease. Doctors do not know the cause of MS, and consequently, the cure eludes them. It is, however, reassuring to know that competent scientists are constantly conducting research to find the cure.

Multiple sclerosis is definitely a serious matter and is not to be taken lightly. However, not only has God given me the ability to be very serious at appropriate times, he has generously blessed me with a healthy sense of humor.

I've written this book with generous amounts of humor and seriousness. Over the years I've been told that laughter is the best medicine, and I wholeheartedly agree that it is. I honestly believe that when living with the frustrations and challenges multiple sclerosis creates, people are doomed from the start if they don't allow for humor at appropriate times. It really is one of God's greatest gifts to us—to experience joy, not constant sadness and negativity.

As may be very true for you, MS has not only affected my life but that of the caregivers (adults and children) as well. To help avoid burnout on their part, your care needs should be evenly allocated among these people. Positive choices we make help to provide the best results for your entire family and care providers. For sure, your well-being is also improved by your choices.

I have done my best to tell my story just as it is, my life with MS. I pray that you gain some beneficial information and a better understanding of this perplexing disease. Especially, I do hope that I have given you examples that convey reasons for hope. I'd like to see every person who has been diagnosed live a full and productive life.

It is also important for you to know that without my trust in God and our gift of prayer, my life would not be joyful, nor would I have a feeling of hope for my future. I would not wish such a sad life for anyone.

At this point, I would like to share bits and pieces of e-mail messages, scriptures, poetry, music, etc. I have found inspirational and uplifting. Like me, these examples contain humor and also serious thoughts.

As positive as I would like to think I am, there are times when my spirit's battery needs a charge—just as my chair does every day.

"Be kinder than necessary because everyone you meet is fighting some kind of battle."

A man carefully explained the four rules he follows every day:

Drink, Steal, Swear, and Lie.
The man then explained these rules.

1. "Drink" from the "everlasting cup" every day.

2. "Steal" a moment to help someone who is in worse shape than you are.

3. "Swear" that you will be a better person today than you were yesterday.

4. And last but not least, when you "lie" down at night, count your blessings.

When you are down to nothing, God is up to something!

A minister parked his car in a no-parking zone in a large city because he was short of time and couldn't find a space with a meter. Then he put a note under the windshield wiper that read:

"I have circled the block ten times. If I don't park here, I'll miss my appointment. Forgive us our trespasses."

When he returned, he found a citation from a police officer along with this note: "I've circled this block for ten years. If I don't give you a ticket I'll lose my job. Lead us not into temptation."

Hymn: Spirit of the Living God

Spirit of the living God, fall afresh on me.
Spirit of the living God, fall afresh on me.
Melt me, mold me, fill me, use me.
Spirit of the living God, fall afresh on me.

E-mail quote: A strong person knows how to keep their life in order. Even with tears in their eyes, they still manage to say "I am okay" with a smile. God is good. Change is coming. God saw your sadness and said, hard times are over.

"Yeah, right, it's not that easy," I protested. "Yes it is," she said. Life is all about choices. When you cut away all the junk, every situation is a choice. You choose how to react to situations. You choose how people affect your mood. You choose to be in a good mood or bad mood. The bottom line: it's your choice how you live your life.

Prayer is one of the best free gifts we receive. There
is no cost, just a lot of reward. Make sure you
pray, and pray believing God will answer.

"Worrying does not empty tomorrow of its
troubles, it empties today of its strength."

Thought for the day:

If God had a refrigerator, your picture would be on it.
If he had a wallet, your photo would be in it.
He sends you flowers every spring.
He sends you a sunrise every morning.
Face it, friend—he is crazy about you.

The following is a scripture we should always
keep present in our hearts. It's greater than ourselves;
we need just to remember the God
we serve and how through HIM, we can do anything:
I can do all things through Christ who strengthens me.
                    Philippians 4:13

I hope this scripture will stick with you not only
today, but also that it will stay with you
throughout the year and forever in your hearts.
There is nothing impossible with God. (Luke 1:37), and

through him and HIS strength, there is
nothing impossible for us.

"Why go to church?"

If you're spiritually alive, you're going to love
this. If you're spiritually dead, you won't want
to read it. If you're spiritually curious, there is still hope.

A church goer wrote a letter to the editor of a
newspaper and complained that it made no
sense to go to church every Sunday. "I've gone
for thirty years now," he wrote, "and in that time I
have heard something like two hundred thousand sermons.

"I've been married for thirty years now. In that time my wife
has cooked some thirty-two thousand meals. But for the life
of me, I cannot recall the entire menu for a single one of those
meals. But I do know this: they all nourished me and gave me
the strength I needed to do my work. If my wife had not given
me these meals, I would be physically dead today. Likewise, if I
had not gone to church for nourishment, I would be spiritually
dead today!" When you are DOWN to nothing, God is UP to
something! Faith sees the invisible, believes the incredible, and
receives the impossible! Thank God for our physical AND our
spiritual nourishment!

May your joys be fulfilled, your dreams be closer,
and your prayers be answered.

I pray that faith enters a new height for you;
I pray that your territory is enlarged. I pray for
peace, healing, health, happiness, prosperity, joy,
true and undying love for God.
(This prayer is meant for each of us).

Psalm 31:24

Be strong and take heart, all you who hope in the LORD.

Remember the five simple rules to be happy:

1. Free your heart from hatred.

2. Free your mind from worries.

3. Live simply.

4. Give more.

5. Expect less.

Psalm 46:1

God is our refuge and strength, an ever-present Help in trouble.

Make the best of what you have; life is truly filled with unpredictable events. God has enabled us to make adjustments.

The song "I Will Survive" by Gloria Gaynor.

I have always liked the title, but I interpret the lyrics in the context of surviving challenges we face (some more serious than others).

Whatever your cross, whatever your pain, there'll always be sunshine, after the rain...

Perhaps you may stumble, perhaps even fall; But he's always ready, to answer your call...

He knows every heartache, sees every tear, a word from his lips, can calm every fear...

Your sorrows may linger, throughout the night,
But suddenly vanish, by early light...

The Savior is waiting, somewhere above, to give
you His grace, and send you His love.

If and when you're dealing with disability, give
yourself credit for trying new things and
accomplishing your goals in new ways.

Don't be so hard on yourself. You deserve a
pat on the back. God wants us to be caring to
others and ourselves.

If I had to describe how MS affects someone, to a person who
knows absolutely nothing about the disease, I would use the anal-
ogy of an unexpected and unwelcome guest in your home (perhaps the in-laws who don't approve of you?). Your family can
support one another and prevent this guest from taking over your
lifestyle and daily routine.

This guest has arrived at your doorstep uninvited and has come
with baggage (i.e., problems). At this point you must make several adjustments affecting your entire family. You, your spouse,
and children may have to take on extra responsibilities in order
to accommodate this uninvited guest. In order to make the best
of the situation, you will have to make choices that will cause less
stress for everyone concerned. The choice is yours. You either go
with the flow and make the best of it, or you choose to make life
miserable for everyone, which benefits no one.

I've often been asked how I manage to keep a positive attitude amid the uncertainties of MS. Other than a loving God, I

have always given credit to my mother. She survived a life filled with hardship and struggle, maintaining a sense of joy and humor. You and I can too! I learned from her example, which spoke volumes. I had little need for books on this topic; I witnessed it for twenty-one years.

At sixty-seven years of age, I feel that God has generously blessed me in many ways throughout my life. Yes, it's true that LIFE HAPPENS—not always according to our liking. However (for example), after the death of my husband Paul, God intervened and reintroduced me to Bob. I have told people that in twenty-one years, Bob and I will celebrate our silver anniversary. Party, party, party! If necessary, I'll sip my margarita(s) through a straw.

"Are you prepared to serve me and to help others?" I do believe God is asking me this question. My answer to this question is "Yes." This book is my attempt at helping others. I do pray that I have achieved my goal.

This is my desire for you:
May the peace, hope, joy, and love of God
be with you!

Made in the USA
Charleston, SC
21 October 2013